Date: 01/25/12

J 551.482 MAC
Macken, JoAnn Early,
Lakes /

WEEKLY WR READER®
EARLY LEARNING LIBRARY

Where on Earth? World Geography

Lakes
by JoAnn Early Macken

Reading consultant: Susan Nations, M.Ed.,
author, literacy coach,
and consultant in literacy development

Learning from Maps

You can learn many things from maps if you know how to read them. This page will help you understand how to read a map.

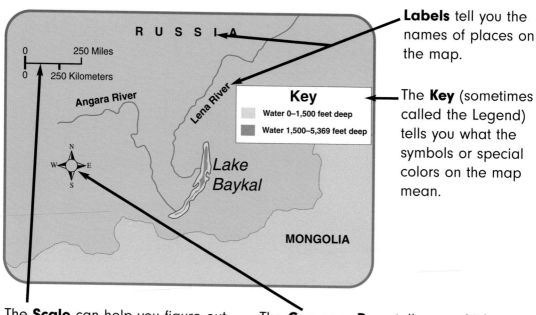

Labels tell you the names of places on the map.

The **Key** (sometimes called the Legend) tells you what the symbols or special colors on the map mean.

The **Scale** can help you figure out how big or far apart places on the map are. For example, a distance of 1 inch (2.5 centimeters) on a map may be hundreds of miles in the real world.

The **Compass Rose** tells you which way is North, South, East, and West.

Table of Contents

Cover and title page: Maligne Lake is located in the Canadian Rocky Mountains.

Like this lake in Canada, some lakes are in places where few people live.

What Is a Lake?

A lake is water with land all around it. A lake can be shallow or deep. Some lakes have fresh water. Other lakes have salty water. Some saltwater lakes are called seas.

Some lakes are too large to see across. Some are nearly small enough to wade from one side to the other. Rivers and streams flow into some lakes. Water flows out of some lakes, too.

This shore is on Lake Michigan. The lake is very large. If you look across it, you cannot see the other side.

Lakes are found all over the world. Lakes supply water, food, and homes for animals and plants. People use lakes for fishing, for traveling, and for fun.

A large lake can change the weather. It can keep the area around it warmer in winter. Sunlight heats the lake's water. The air above and near it stays warm for a long time. In summer, cool air over the lake helps cool the area around it.

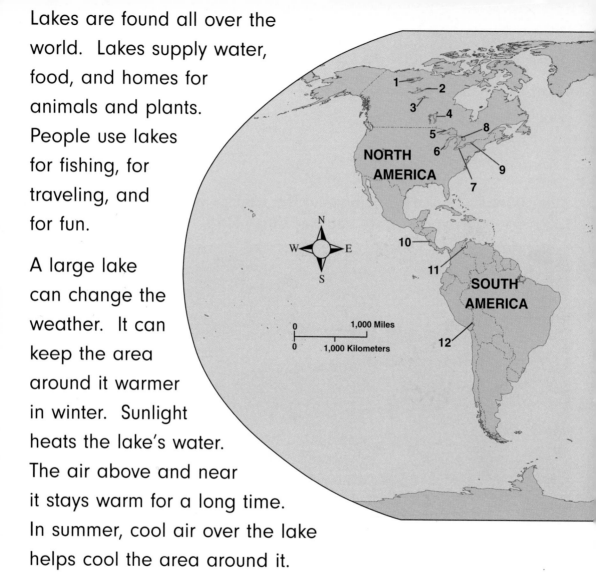

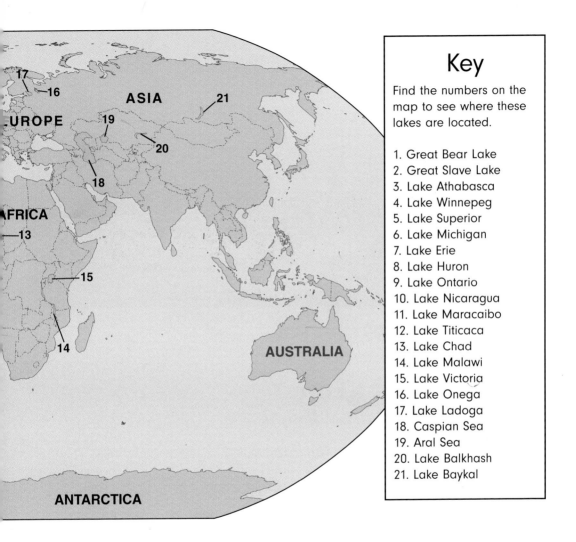

ASIA 21

EUROPE 19

17
16

20

AFRICA
13

18

15

14

AUSTRALIA

ANTARCTICA

Key

Find the numbers on the map to see where these lakes are located.

1. Great Bear Lake
2. Great Slave Lake
3. Lake Athabasca
4. Lake Winnepeg
5. Lake Superior
6. Lake Michigan
7. Lake Erie
8. Lake Huron
9. Lake Ontario
10. Lake Nicaragua
11. Lake Maracaibo
12. Lake Titicaca
13. Lake Chad
14. Lake Malawi
15. Lake Victoria
16. Lake Onega
17. Lake Ladoga
18. Caspian Sea
19. Aral Sea
20. Lake Balkhash
21. Lake Baykal

This map shows the largest lakes in the world.

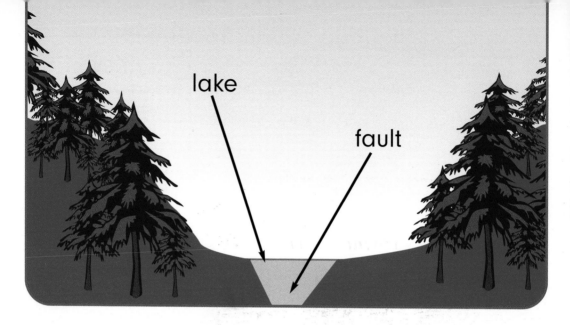

lake

fault

Lakes can form along faults in the earth.

How Do Lakes Form?

An earthquake can cause huge cracks in land, called **faults**. Rain and snow fill the faults, forming lakes.

Sometimes, the land on one side of a fault is higher than the other side. Water may flow to the lower side. The water collected can cover the ground on the lower side and form a lake.

Wind can **carve**, or dig, a hole in the land. The hole may become deep enough to reach water that is underground. This water fills the hole, forming a lake. Sometimes, flowing water **seeps**, or drips, into the ground. The water carves out a space beneath the ground and forms an underground lake.

Some lakes can be found under the ground.

Thousands of years ago, this volcano in Oregon exploded. The crater filled with rain and snow, creating Crater Lake.

The top of a volcano can blow off or cave in. A **crater**, or bowl-shaped hole, is left behind. When the hole fills with rain or snow, a lake is formed.

If a meteor strikes Earth, it can leave a deep hole in the ground. The hole may fill with water, becoming a lake.

Rivers often wind back and forth. They even flow in U-shaped loops. Sometimes, a river floods. The water flows across the land inside the loop. The water makes a new, straight path for the river. Water stops flowing all the way around the loop. The loop gets cut off from the river and becomes a lake. If more water does not flow into it, the lake may disappear.

This U-shaped lake in California was once part of a river. The river now flows past the lake in a straight path.

After a beaver built a dam, this lake formed in Wyoming. The Teton Mountains are reflected in the lake's water.

A tree can fall across a stream and stop the flow of water. A lake will form behind the tree. A beaver may build a dam from logs, rocks, and mud. The dam will stop the water and create a lake. A landslide of rocks and dirt can also block a river. A lake may form behind the blockage.

Sometimes, a reef or a sandbar can cut off part of an ocean. The part that is cut off becomes a lake. It has salty water, just like the ocean. A lake will stay salty if no water flows out. The water becomes more salty as the lake dries up.

The Great Salt Lake is in Utah. Rivers flow into the lake. When they bring less water, the lake becomes smaller. As the water dries up, it leaves salt behind.

This glacier has left low spots in the land. Water has filled the spot here, forming a lake.

Many lakes began as ice. Huge rivers of ice called **glaciers** move slowly over land. Glaciers also carry rocks and sand. As they slide, they carve and scrape the land. They make holes, ridges, and grooves. Melting ice fills the low spots. Thousands of years ago, glaciers formed the Great Lakes in North America.

People and Lakes

People build dams on rivers. The dams create lakes. The water is used for watering crops, drinking, and boating. The water also provides power. Small amounts of water pass through a dam. This water flows quickly past special wheels, causing them to spin. The spinning motion creates electricity. Dams also help control flooding by holding back extra water.

This dam has created a large lake behind it.

15

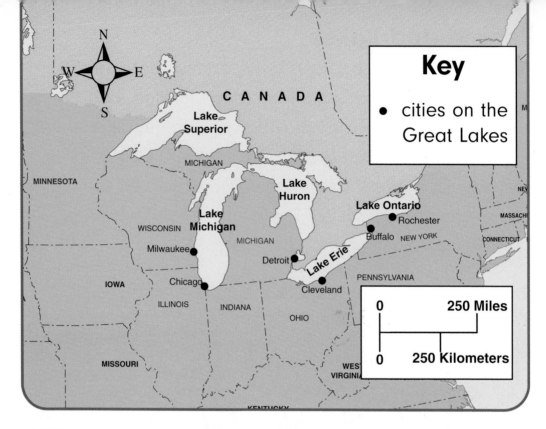

Millions of people live near the five Great Lakes.

The five Great Lakes hold one-fifth of the fresh water in the world. Lake Superior is the world's largest freshwater lake. Many people live in cities built on the shores of the lakes.

The Life of a Lake

In the deepest part of a lake, the water is cold and dark. Dead plants and animals drift down there. Fish called bottom-feeders eat them. In the middle layers, big fish may eat smaller fish. In shallow water, sunlight shines through the water. Algae and other plants grow there.

This carp is feeding just beneath the surface of a lake.

This caribou in Alaska visits a lake to drink water.

Some plants and animals live near the top of the water. They are very tiny. Fish, birds, and turtles eat them. Ducks paddle across the lake. Many animals come to the shore to drink. Eagles and other birds of prey circle in the sky above, looking for fish to catch.

Lakes are always changing. Water flowing into a lake can make it grow larger. Falling rain and snow add more water. Water flowing out of a lake can make it become smaller. A river flowing out of a lake can wear down the land there. Then, even more water leaks out. Over time, if very little rain falls, a lake can dry up.

When very little rain fell, this lake in Arizona dried up.

A river can carry sand and mud into a lake. The sand and mud settle on the bottom. Falling leaves also settle on the bottom. Dust and animal bones build up there. Plants grow along the edges of the lake. After awhile, plants also grow in the middle of the lake. They grow on the bottom, too. The lake gets filled. It becomes smaller and smaller. Over time, it dries up and disappears.

Plants and other things can fill up a lake. Then, it may disappear.

Spotlight: Lake Baykal

Lake Baykal is in Russia. It is the deepest lake on Earth. It may also be the oldest. It holds more fresh water than any other lake. It fills a huge crack in the ground. More than three hundred rivers flow into the lake.

This map shows how deep Lake Baykal is in different areas.

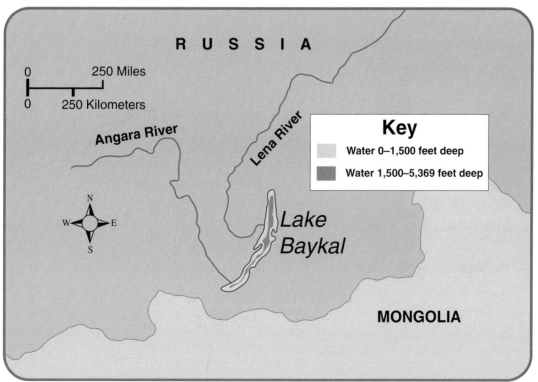

RUSSIA

0   250 Miles

0   250 Kilometers

Angara River

Lena River

Key

Water 0–1,500 feet deep

Water 1,500–5,369 feet deep

N W E S

Lake Baykal

MONGOLIA

Glossary

crater — a hole shaped like a bowl, such as those at the top of a mountain or on the Moon

faults — breaks in rock layers caused by a shifting of Earth's crust, or outer layer

landslide — a large pile of loose rocks and earth that falls down a hill or mountain

meteor — a small body from outer space that falls to Earth

reef — a strip of rock, coral, or sand near the surface of a body of water

sandbar — a ridge of sand in a body of water

shallow — not deep

volcano — a hole in Earth's crust where lava, rocks, and ashes flow from inside Earth

For More Information

Books

Icebergs and Glaciers. Seymour Simon (Mulberry Books)

If You Want to See a Caribou. Phyllis Root (Houghton Mifflin)

Lakes. Water Habitats (series). JoAnn Early Macken
    (Weekly Reader Early Learning Library)

Water in Rivers and Lakes. Isaac Nadeau (PowerKids Press)

What's in the Pond? Anne Hunter (Houghton Mifflin)

What's Inside Lakes? Jane Kelly Kosek (PowerKids Press)

Web Sites

Fish of the Great Lakes
www.seagrant.wisc.edu/greatlakesfish/framefish.html
See pictures and learn about the fish in the Great Lakes.

Ponds and Lakes
mbgnet.mobot.org/fresh
See the Great Lakes from space, learn how ponds
develop, and more.

Index

About the Author

JoAnn Early Macken is the author of two rhyming picture books, *Sing-Along Song* and *Cats on Judy*, and more than eighty nonfiction books for children. Her poems have appeared in several children's magazines. A graduate of the M.F.A. in Writing for Children and Young Adults Program at Vermont College, she lives in Wisconsin with her husband and their two sons.

Please visit our web site at: www.earlyliteracy.cc
For a free color catalog describing Weekly Reader®
Early Learning Library's list of high-quality books,
call 1-877-445-5824 (USA) or 1-800-387-3178 (Canada).
Weekly Reader® Early Learning Library's fax: (414) 336-0164.

Library of Congress Cataloging-in-Publication Data

Macken, JoAnn Early, 1953–
    Lakes / JoAnn Early Macken.
        p. cm. — (Where on earth? world geography)
    Includes bibliographical references and index.
    ISBN 0-8368-6394-1 (lib. bdg.)
    ISBN 0-8368-6401-8 (softcover)
    1. Lakes—Juvenile literature. I. Title.
    GB1603.8.M33   2006
    551.48'2—dc22   2005025575

This edition first published in 2006 by
Weekly Reader® Early Learning Library
A Member of the WRC Media Family of Companies
330 West Olive Street, Suite 100
Milwaukee, WI 53212 USA

Copyright © 2006 by Weekly Reader® Early Learning Library
Editors: Jim Mezzanotte and Barbara Kiely Miller
Art direction: Tammy West
Cover design and page layout: Kami Strunsee
Picture research: Diane Laska-Swanke

Picture credits: Cover, title, © Tom and Pat Leeson; pp. 2, 6-7, 8, 16, 21 Kami Strunsee/© Weekly Reader Early Learning Library, 2006; p. 4 © David Noton/naturepl.com; p. 5 © James P. Rowan; p. 9 © Albert J. Copley/Visuals Unlimited; pp. 10, 14 © Marli Miller/Visuals Unlimited; p. 11 © Dane Johnson/Visuals Unlimited; p. 12 © Jeff Foott/naturepl.com; pp. 13, 15 © John Sohlden/Visuals Unlimited; p. 17 © Tim Martin/naturepl.com; p. 18 © Patrick J. Endres/Visuals Unlimited; p. 19 © Henry Robison/Visuals Unlimited; p. 20 © Scott Berner/Visuals Unlimited

Printed in the United States of America

1 2 3 4 5 6 7 8 9 10 09 08 07 06